I0828192

THIS BOOK BELONGS TO:

WELCOME
TO NEBRASKA
GREAT SEAL OF THE STATE OF NEBRASKA
EQUALITY
BEFORE
THE LAW
MARCH 1ST 1867

Dedicated to all the explorers.

ISBN 978-1-970416-03-9

www.joeysavestheday.com

Mimi Books™ Publishing

A Mimi Book

Nebraska got its name from the Otoe word "Nebrathka," which means "flat water." Early explorers used the word to describe the wide, calm Platte River that flows across the region. The river was so important to the land and the people who lived there that its name inspired the name of the state.

Platte River

Nebraska has a long history that begins with Native American nations who lived along its wide rivers, open prairies, and rolling plains for thousands of years. Tribes such as the Omaha, Ponca, Otoe-Missouria, and Pawnee built strong communities across the region. In the 1800s, explorers, traders, and later settlers arrived, many traveling along famous trails like the Oregon and Mormon Trails.

Nebraska was the thirty-seventh state to join the Union. It officially became a state on March 1, 1867.

Nebraska is located in the Midwestern United States. It is bordered by South Dakota, Iowa, Missouri, Kansas, Colorado, and Wyoming.

Lincoln is the capital of Nebraska. It officially became the capital in 1867.

Lincoln, Nebraska, has an estimated population of about 300,600 people.

Nebraska is the sixteenth largest state in the United States by area.

16th

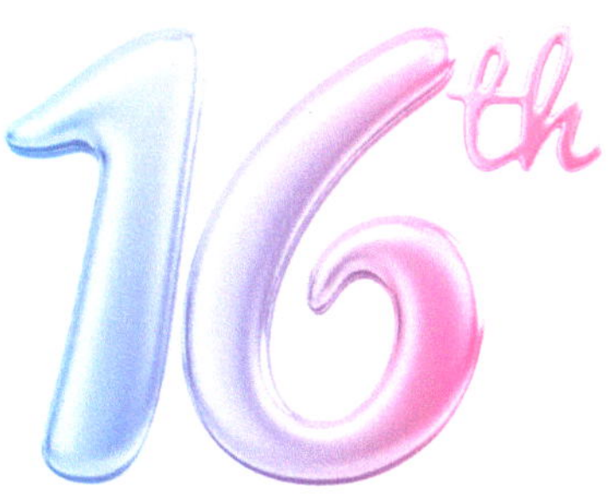

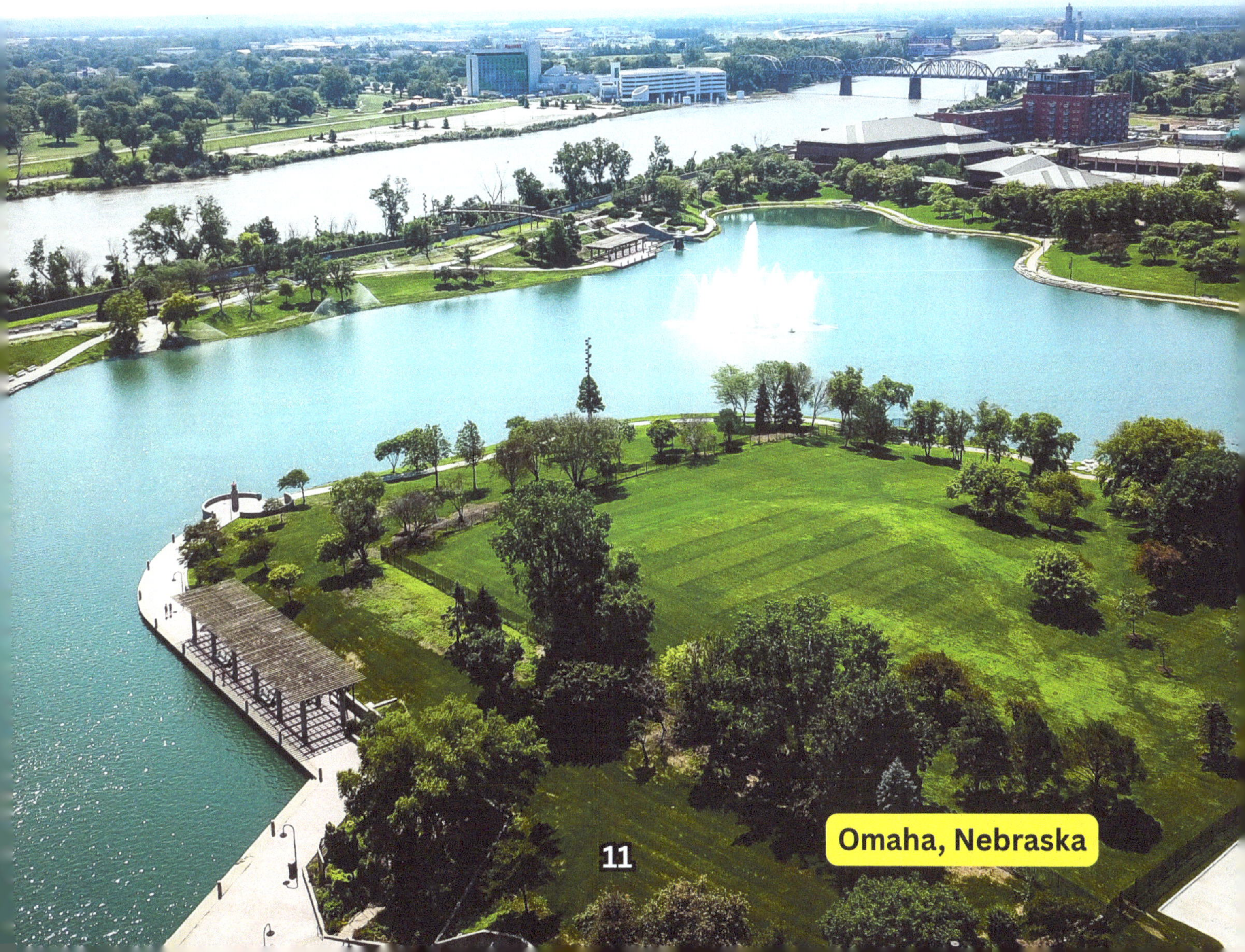

Omaha, Nebraska

There are approximately 2,005,400 people residing in the state of Nebraska.

Kearney, Nebraska

Buffalo Bill Cody, a famous showman of the American West, is remembered at Buffalo Bill Ranch State Historical Park in North Platte, Nebraska. His big white house, called the "Second Empire" mansion, still stands with its tall windows and wide porches. The rooms are filled with old furniture, costumes, and tools that show what life was like when Buffalo Bill created his world-famous Wild West shows.

Nebraska is the birthplace of Kool-Aid! This bright, fruity drink was invented in Hastings, Nebraska, by a man named Edwin Perkins. He wanted to make a fun, affordable drink mix that families could enjoy together. Today, kids all over the country still love Kool-Aid, and Nebraska celebrates it every year with a big, colorful festival.

NEBRASKA

There are 93 counties in Nebraska.

Here is a list of twenty of those counties:

Adams	Cass	Dundy	Greeley
Banner	Cherry	Fillmore	Hall
Boone Box	Custer	Franklin	Harlan
Butte	Dakota	Gage	Keith
Butler	Dawson	Garden	York

Smith Falls is Nebraska's tallest waterfall, gently spilling over a rocky cliff into a cool, shallow pool. A wooden boardwalk leads kids right up to the falls, where they can feel the light mist and hear the soft splash of the water. The area around the falls was shaped by the Niobrara River over thousands of years, creating a peaceful canyon filled with plants and wildlife.

Smith Falls State Park

One of the most important moments in Nebraska's history is the completion of the Transcontinental Railroad in 1869. This major project brought thousands of workers and new families to the region, helping small towns grow into busy communities across the Great Plains. The railroad connected the East Coast to the West Coast, making travel faster and opening new opportunities for trade, farming, and business.

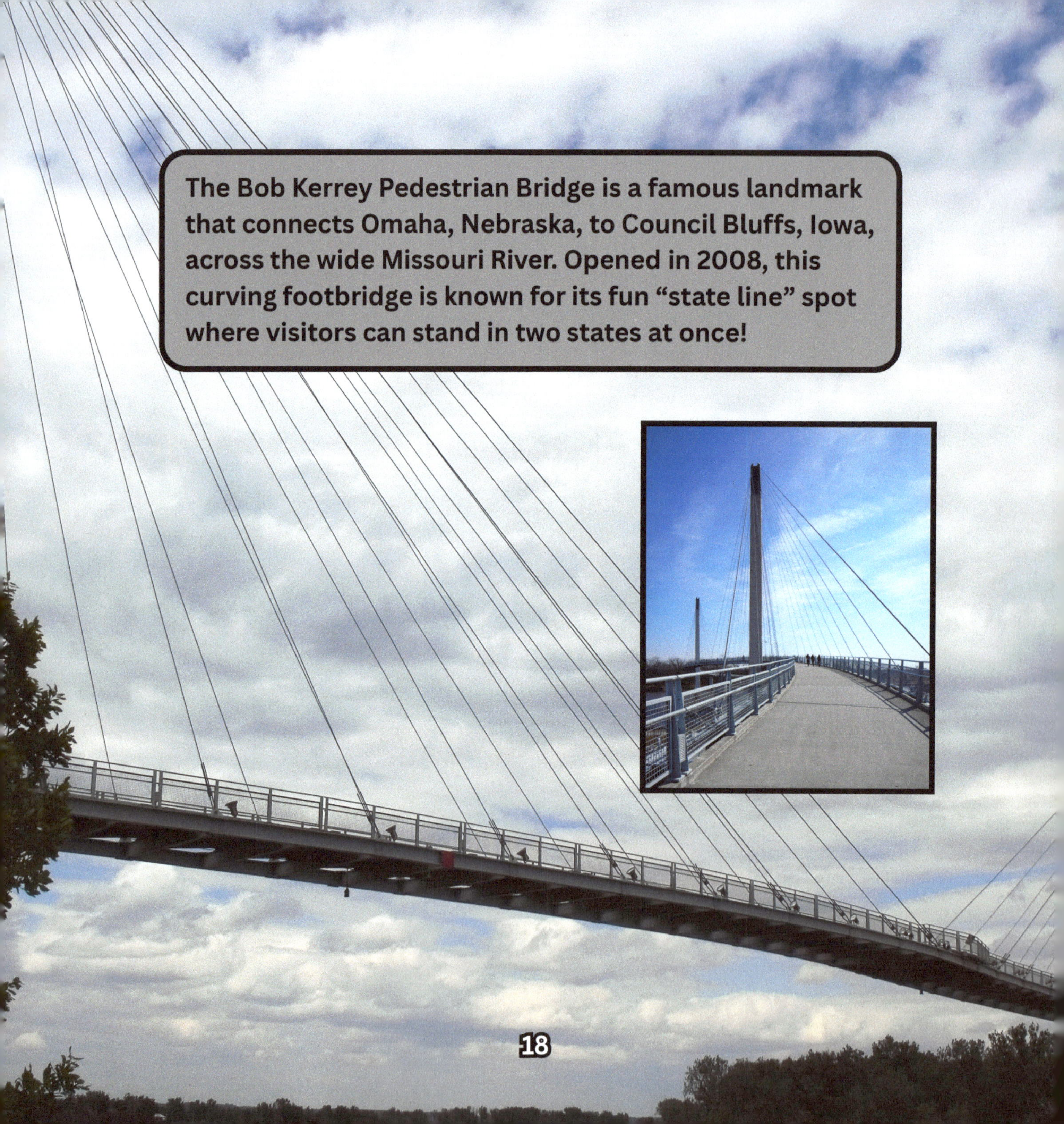

The Bob Kerrey Pedestrian Bridge is a famous landmark that connects Omaha, Nebraska, to Council Bluffs, Iowa, across the wide Missouri River. Opened in 2008, this curving footbridge is known for its fun “state line” spot where visitors can stand in two states at once!

The Nebraska state bird is the Western Meadowlark. It was chosen as the state bird in 1929.

The official state flower of Nebraska is the Goldenrod. It was chosen as the state flower in 1895.

A couple of Nebraska's nicknames include the Cornhusker State and the Beef State.

-ER ST8

THE

ST8

Nebraska's state motto is "Equality Before the Law." It was adopted in 1867.

What "Equality Before the Law" Means:

- The motto shows that everyone should be treated fairly, no matter who they are.
- It reflects Nebraska's belief that all people deserve the same rights and protections under the law.

Put together, the motto is saying:
Nebraska believes in fairness, justice, and equal treatment for all people.

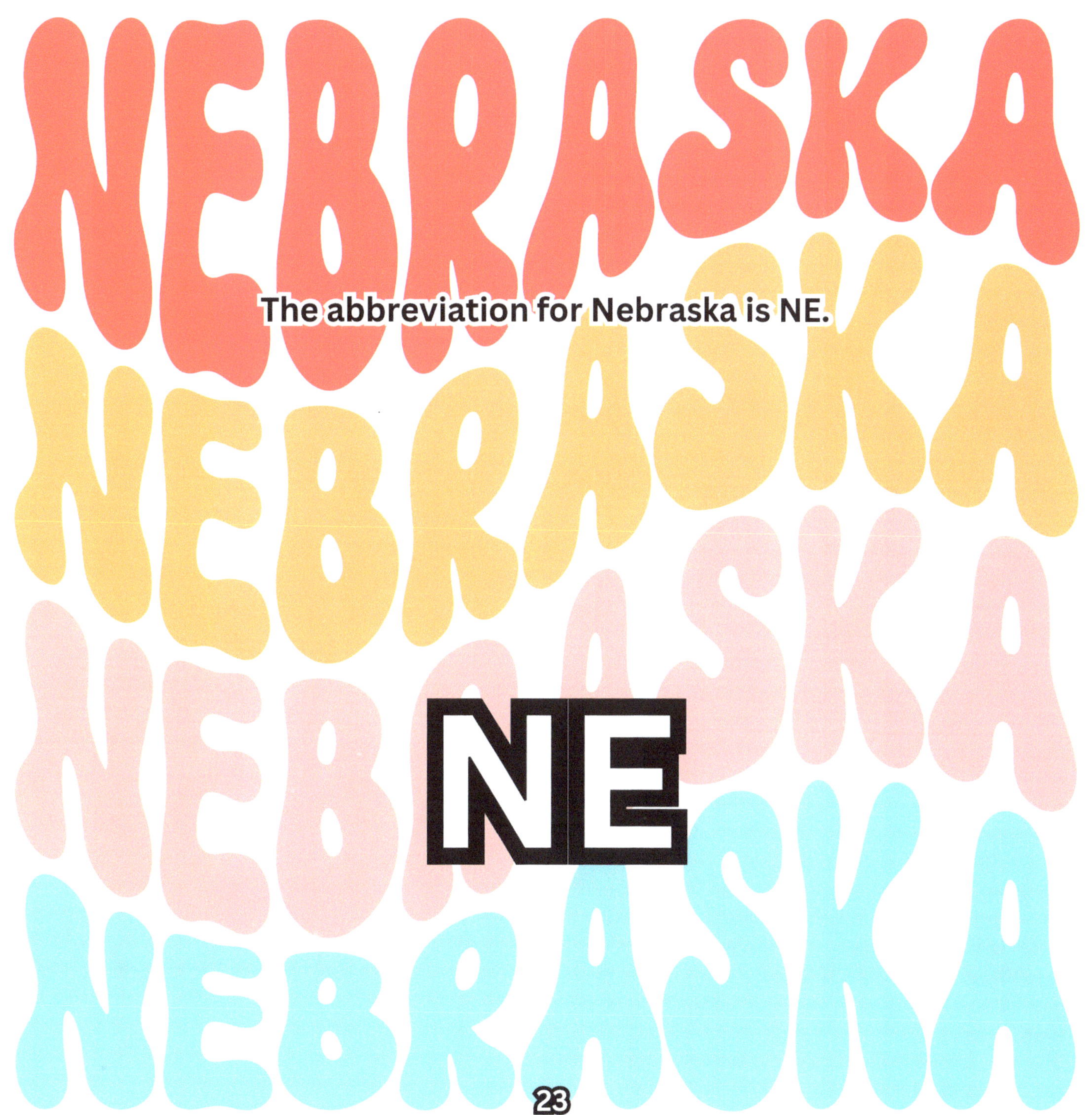
NEBRASKA
NEBRASKA
NEBRASKA
NEBRASKA
The abbreviation for Nebraska is NE.
NE

Nebraska's state flag was officially adopted in 1925.

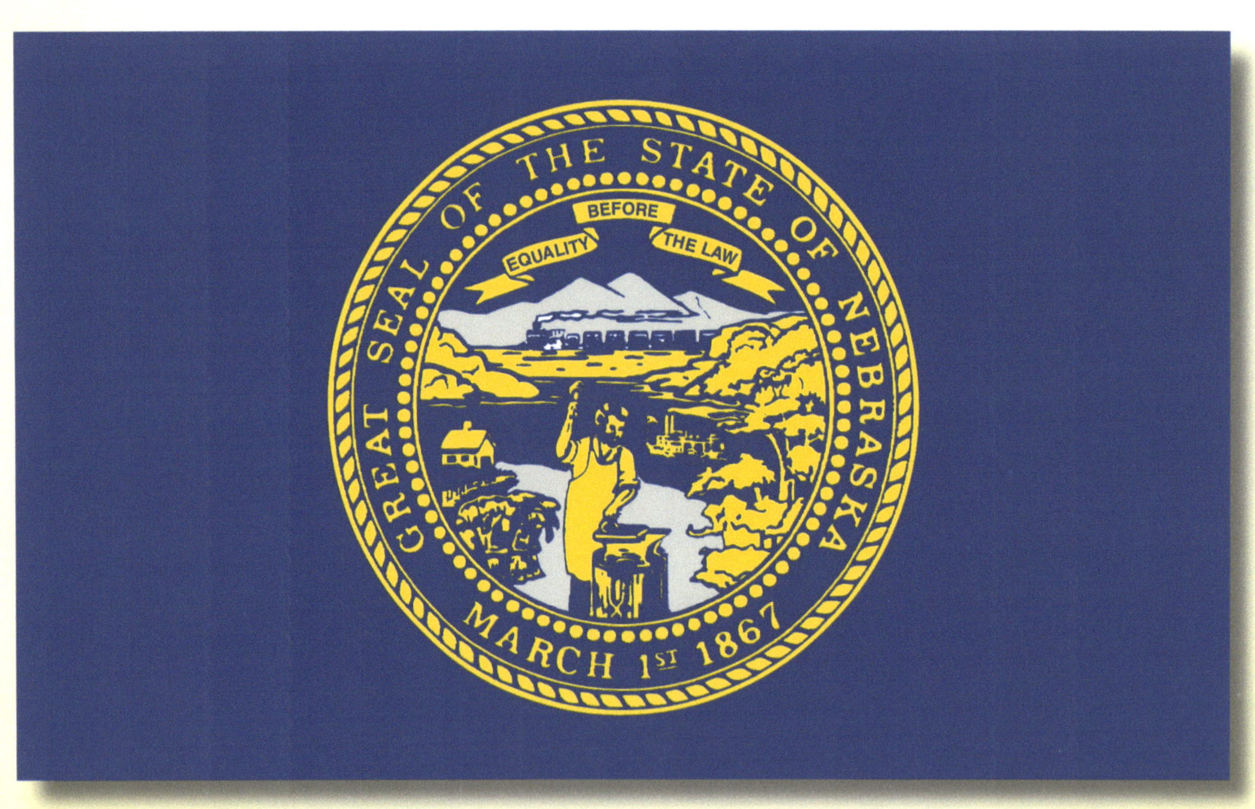

Some crops grown in Nebraska are corn, soybeans, wheat, and hay.

Some animals that live in Nebraska are white-tailed deer, coyotes, red foxes, prairie dogs, and wild turkeys.

Nebraska experiences a wide range of temperatures throughout the year. The hottest temperature ever recorded in the state was 118 degrees Fahrenheit, measured in Minden on July 24, 1936. In contrast, the coldest temperature documented was −47 degrees Fahrenheit, recorded in Camp Clarke on February 12, 1899.

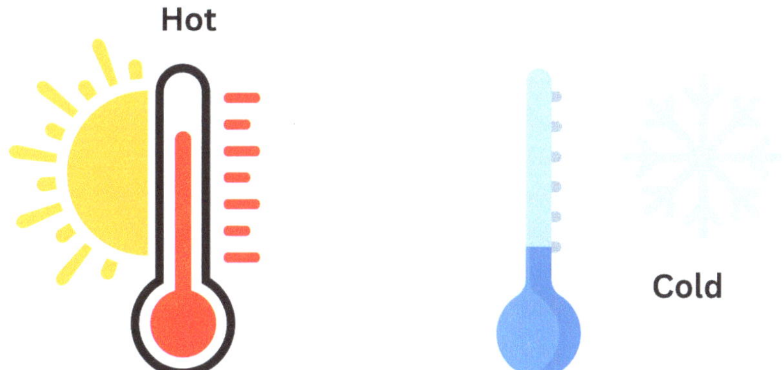

The Lincoln Children's Zoo in Lincoln is a wonderful place to explore, with animals from all around the world. Kids can see cheetahs, red pandas, giraffes, penguins, and playful primates, along with colorful birds and reptiles.

George Beadle was a scientist from Nebraska who studied how genes work. His discoveries helped people understand how traits are passed from parents to their children. People remember him for his important research and his big contributions to modern genetics.

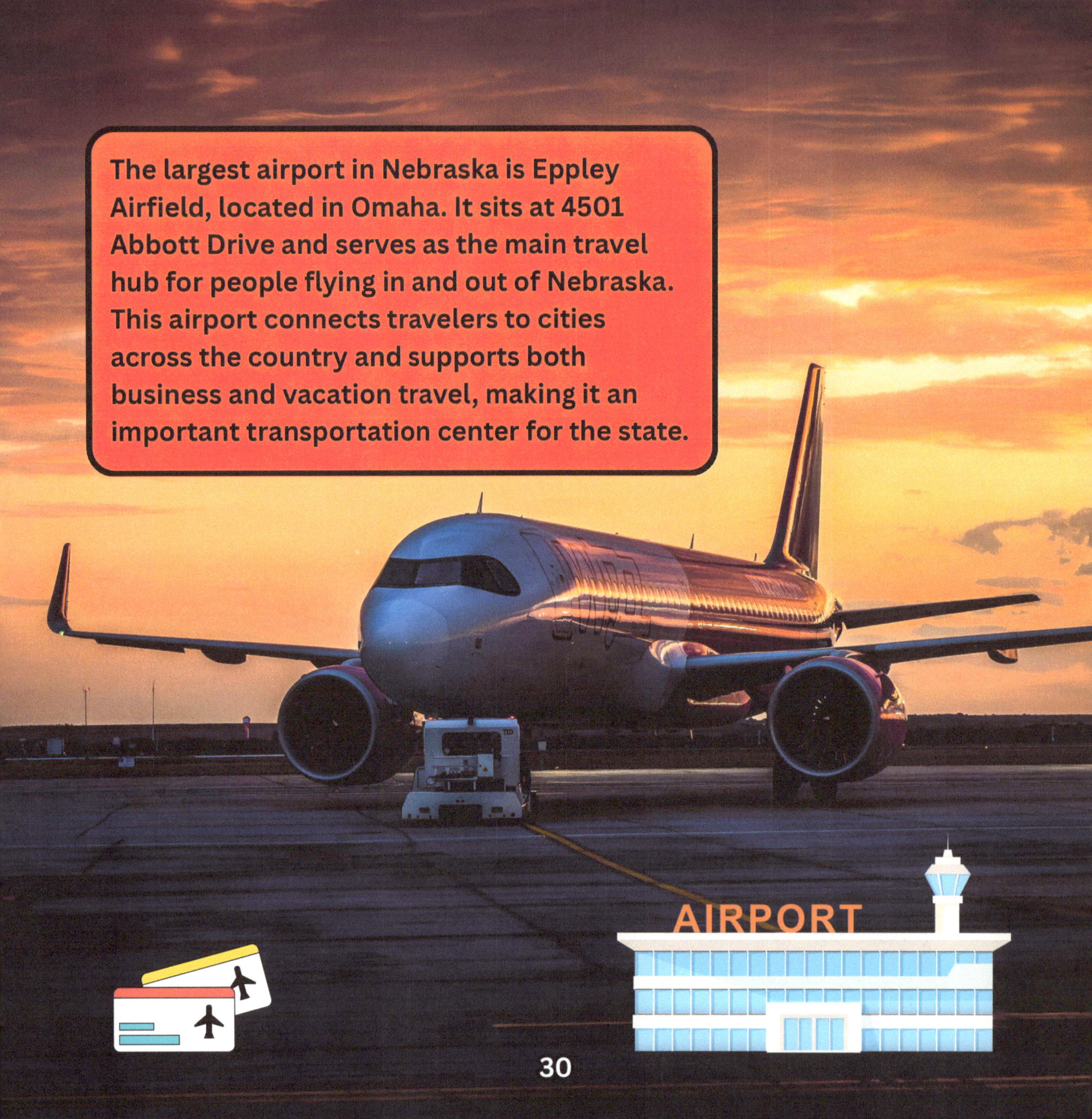

The largest airport in Nebraska is Eppley Airfield, located in Omaha. It sits at 4501 Abbott Drive and serves as the main travel hub for people flying in and out of Nebraska. This airport connects travelers to cities across the country and supports both business and vacation travel, making it an important transportation center for the state.

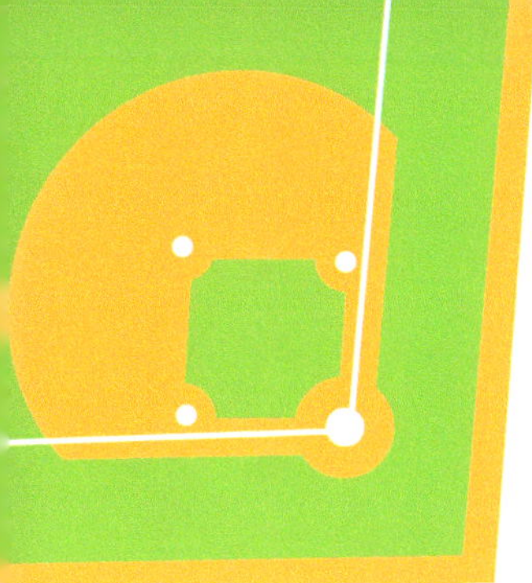

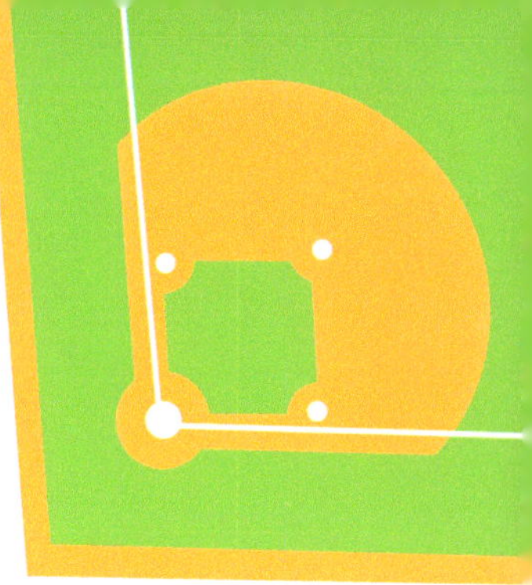

The Omaha Storm Chasers are a professional baseball team based in Omaha, one of Nebraska's largest and most well-known cities. They play their home games at Werner Park, a bright and welcoming ballpark known for its fun atmosphere, family-friendly events, and great views of the field. The Storm Chasers have helped many talented players grow their skills over the years, giving them a place to shine as they work toward making baseball history.

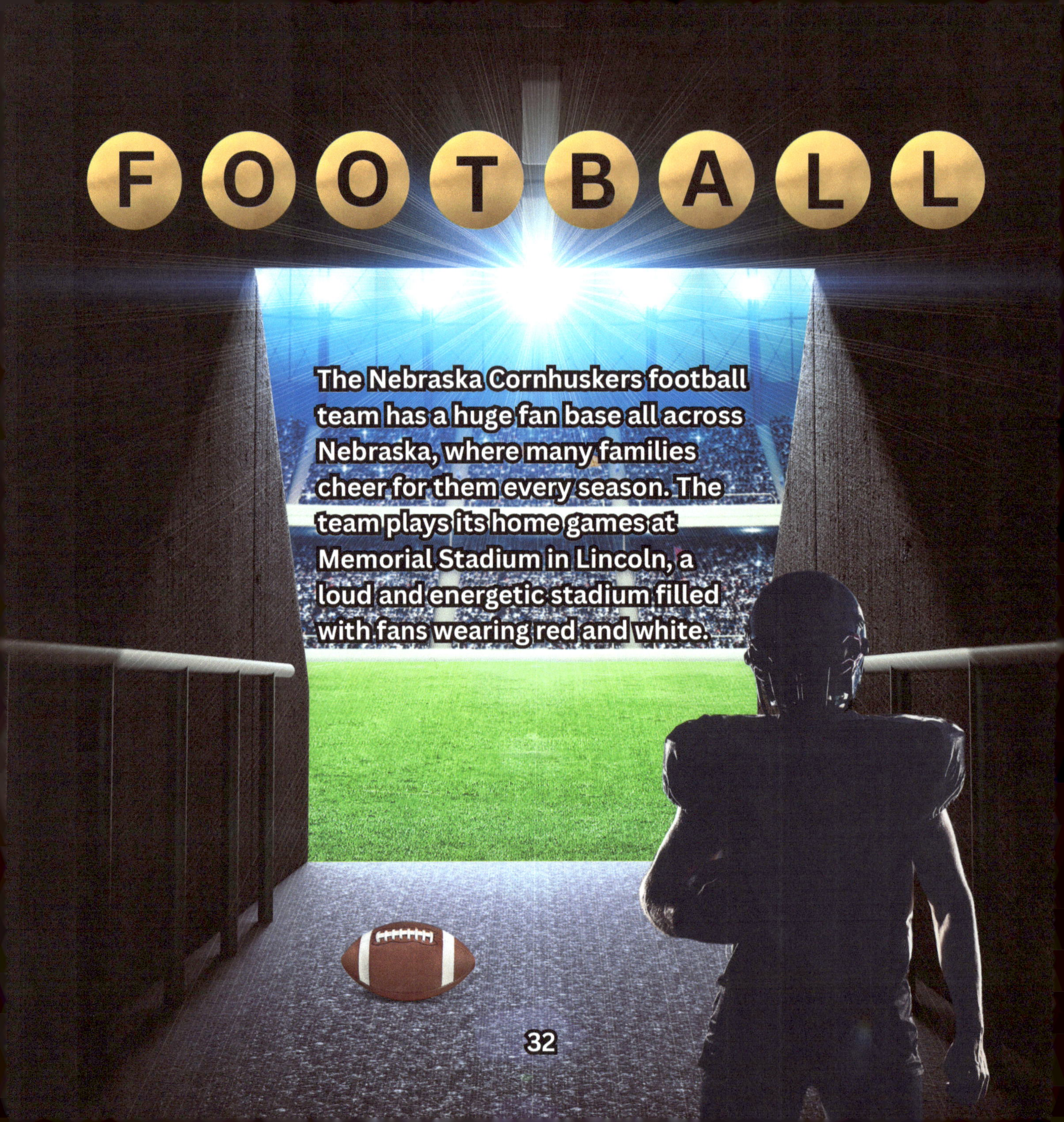

FOOTBALL

The Nebraska Cornhuskers football team has a huge fan base all across Nebraska, where many families cheer for them every season. The team plays its home games at Memorial Stadium in Lincoln, a loud and energetic stadium filled with fans wearing red and white.

The eastern cottonwood is Nebraska's state tree. It's known for its tall trunk, wide branches, and shimmering heart-shaped leaves that rustle softly in the wind. The cottonwood was officially adopted as the state tree in 1972, and its strength and beauty have made it a lasting symbol of Nebraska's natural landscapes.

The channel catfish is Nebraska's state fish. It's a smooth-skinned fish with whisker-like barbels, a wide mouth, and a gentle, rounded shape that makes it easy to recognize in rivers and lakes. The channel catfish was officially adopted as the state fish in 1997, and it's a familiar sight in Nebraska's freshwater habitats.

Can you name these?

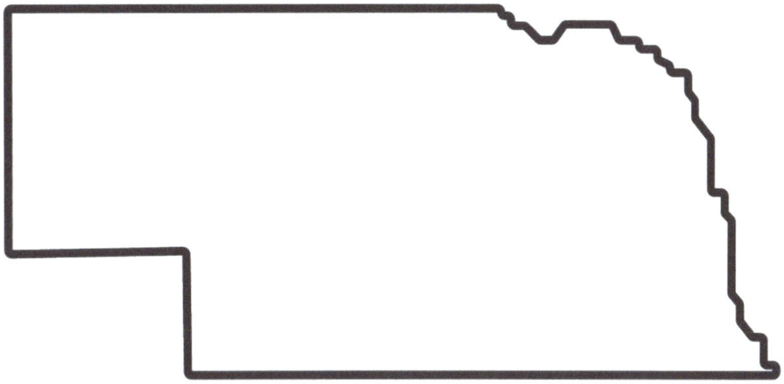

I hope you enjoyed learning about Nebraska.

To explore fun facts about the other 49 states, visit my website at www.joeysavestheday.com. You'll also find a wide variety of homeschool resources to support joyful learning at home. If you enjoyed this book, I would be grateful if you left a review. Your feedback truly helps. Thank you for your support!

Check out these other interesting books in the 50 States Fact Books Series!

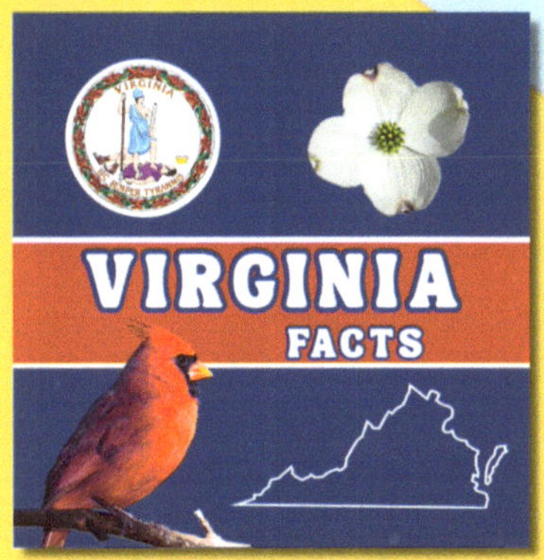

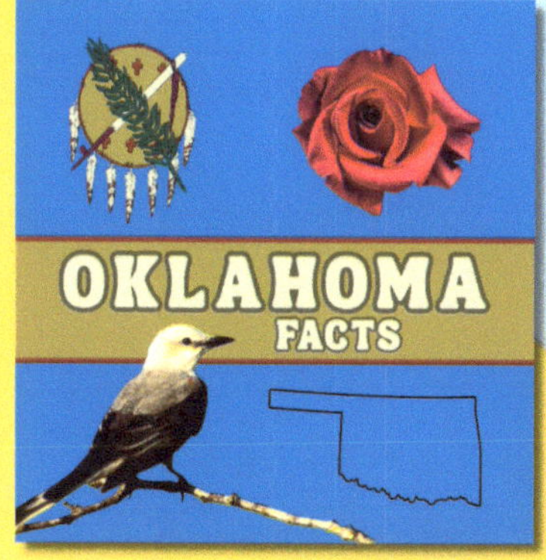

www.mimibooks.com

www.ingramcontent.com/pod-product-compliance
Lightning Source LLC
LaVergne TN
LVHW070200110826
845147LV00002B/459